Sherborne Old C...

Peter White

CONTENTS

Tour of the Castle

OVERVIEW AND SETTING

Sherborne Old Castle was built less than a mile from the monastery of Sherborne, then one of the richest religious houses in southern England. The castle was ideally located to control the old road from London, which passed Sarum (Salisbury), Shaftesbury and Sherborne, en route to Exeter and the seaports of Devon and Cornwall.

Its immediate setting when built was very different to that now: the low hill upon which it stands then formed the tip of a promontory surrounded by a mere, or shallow lake, probably created deliberately and fed by two streams still flowing today. The stream to the south now feeds the lake of the new castle from the east; downstream from the lake it is crossed by Dynney Bridge. By land the castle could be reached only along the promontory from the east; otherwise it was accessed via fords and bridges (see page 26). By the 16th century the mere had silted up to form marshy ground and over time it turned into water meadows. In the mid 19th century the new railway embankment disrupted the approach from the north.

It is likely that the castle site was originally a domed hill. Bishop Roger's workmen levelled it, creating a building platform that formed the bailey, which they enclosed with a curtain wall with three gates. Within the bailey four palatial ranges surrounded a square courtyard. Attached to the west range, and dominating the site, was the massive great tower that provided secure apartments for the bishop and his immediate household. This tower could be defended, similarly

Above: View looking east over the edge of the town towards Sherborne Old Castle, left, and the new castle, right. The lake between them was formed from the remains of the mere, which originally largely surrounded the old castle

Below: A beak-head, a Norman architectural decoration, which once adorned Bishop Roger's castle

Facing page: The castle ruins seen from across the lake to the south

3

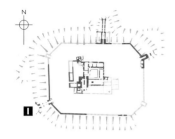

to a castle keep. Beside the east range was a detached kitchen. Later a courtyard was added to the west of the original complex. Just outside the eastern curtain wall, but still within the protective shield of the mere, were buildings forming an outer court, with a chapel, stabling and lodgings for those not permitted to enter the bailey. On the other side of the thin arm of the mere, to the south, was an extensive deer park, important to the household for both sport and food.

In the 1640s, during the Civil War, two earthwork bastions were built just outside the curtain wall by the Royalist defenders of the castle, facing east and west, to mount artillery.

■ SOUTH-WEST GATEHOUSE

The ditch outside the curtain wall is seen at its most impressive from the south-west gatehouse bridge. Originally the bridge was solid stone (its stone abutments and pier survive), with a section of timber that could be removed in case of attack, as the drawbridge had yet to be invented. The timber section was later altered on the inner side to form a drawbridge; the pit for its counterbalance can still clearly be seen.

The south-west gatehouse was always the main entrance to the castle. It would have been used by the high-ranking

Above: An iron spur, dating from the mid 17th century, found at Sherborne, and possibly lost during the Civil War. Such spurs were known at the time as 'Scotch' spurs

Right: A reconstruction drawing of the south-west gatehouse as first built, in about 1130. The bridge had a timber section which, in the case of attack, could be removed, rendering the bridge uncrossable

Below: The castle ditch looking towards the south-west

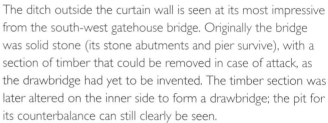

residents and their visitors. The gate arch and, at first-floor
level, the large round-headed window and the two smaller
ones in the side walls are original. Above these was a single
upper chamber with a sloping roof rising from nearly floor level
to the height of the tower façade. The line of this original roof
can just be seen as grooves in the two short angles of wall on
the inner side of the gatehouse. In the 16th century Sir Walter
Ralegh converted the gatehouse into lodgings for his caretaker,
John Meere. He removed the steeply pitched roof and divided
the upper chamber into two upper floors, creating the
square-headed windows and the chimney seen today.

The gate passage vaulting has gone, allowing a view of the
fireplaces, stair and arrangement of the upper floors as created
by Ralegh. Beyond the jambs for the great outer doors, and
the hole for the drawbar to secure them, is a small porter's
lodge. The stair to the upper chambers was accessed via a
doorway inside the bailey. It is now blocked.

Flanking the gatehouse are the two best-preserved lengths
of curtain wall. They survive to the height of the wall walk,
indicated by the original doorways which lead out on each side
of the tower. When built, the curtain wall would have had a
crenellated parapet.

Above: The south-west gatehouse
seen from within the west range.
Probably in the 14th century a
doorway was created in the west
range, allowing visitors to enter
the castle on this side
Left: A reconstruction drawing of the
south-west gatehouse in about 1595,
after Sir Walter Ralegh had converted
it into living quarters for his caretaker
Below: The south-west gatehouse,
always the main entrance to
the castle, seen from the bridge
over the ditch

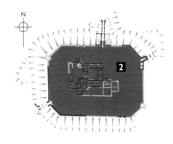

Below: A door jamb from Roger's castle adorned with a beak-head

Bottom: A reconstruction drawing of the castle when first built, c.1130, when the mere still largely surrounded the site. To the south (top) is Roger's hunting lodge across the mere, and to the east (left) is the outer court

2 BAILEY

The bailey is an area of nearly four acres. To create this extensive building platform, Roger's workmen levelled what was probably originally a domed hill, using only hand-held tools. It was both a major feat and a significant element of Roger's grand design. It emphasized the residential nature of Sherborne at a time when elsewhere magnates were building castles with steeply sloping ground for their defence.

The bailey forms an elongated octagon, which Roger's workmen enclosed with a deep, dry ditch. On the outer side of the ditch they built up a bank, or counterscarp, and on its inner side a battlemented curtain wall about 36ft (11m) high, with four towers, two of which had gates. On the north side was a third gate, a unique pedestrian entrance within a barbican (defensive enclosure) that functioned as a storage yard leading to the fishponds of the mere.

The principal domestic buildings were at the centre of the bailey and were dominated by the massive residential great tower. They surrounded and concealed from the bailey an inner courtyard. When first built the buildings and inner courtyard could only be accessed from the bailey via a door at the east end of the great hall, which formed the south range. This innovative plan introduced by Roger provided security and privacy. Later a second access to the buildings and inner courtyard was created from the west (see page 10).

The central complex of buildings, and that part of the bailey between it and the south-west gatehouse, was reserved for important residents and visitors. There would have been buildings against the curtain wall, but quite soon after Roger's time additional buildings, probably lodgings, were constructed, attached to the south-west face of the great tower.

Bishop Roger

Roger, a priest from Normandy, became one of the most influential men in 12th-century England.

Roger was born in or near Caen in the late 1060s and met the future Henry I, the youngest son of William the Conqueror, when Henry was fighting his brother in Normandy. Henry so valued Roger's abilities that, shortly after becoming King of England in 1100, he made Roger chancellor, the most senior official in his household. Henry also wanted to make him Bishop of Sarum (Salisbury), but Lanfranc, Archbishop of Canterbury, blocked Roger's appointment until 1107.

Roger accumulated power and became, in practice, justiciar – a title that only came into use some 50 years later, but which described a role much greater than that of chancellor, with financial and judicial responsibilities.

By 1110 Roger was managing the king's finances, which were based at the Treasury in Winchester. He consolidated the audit procedures of the royal household using counters on a chequered cloth – the exchequer – and began the system of keeping records on parchment (the archive known today as the Pipe Rolls).

Roger's reforms established for the first time a system of government distinct from the royal household. His contemporary William of Malmesbury noted that the king, whether abroad or not,

Left: A 15th-century illustration of the exchequer of Ireland at work. It was probably Roger who brought this system of counting upon a chequered cloth from France to Henry's Treasury

Below: A carved head from Roger's cathedral at Sarum

'committed to his [Roger's] care the administration of the whole kingdom'. Roger worked closely with Henry's queen, Matilda, and after her death in 1118 he was effectively vice-regent.

As Bishop of Sarum Roger was titular abbot of the religious houses in this diocese: Sherborne until 1122, when he made it an independent abbey, and both Abbotsbury and Malmesbury until his death. In 1121 he assisted in Henry's foundation of Reading Abbey. He used his power to good effect, creating magnificent buildings and founding a school, or secular chapter, at Sarum. Here administrators were trained, in cooperation with clergy from Laon, where he had sent his nephews – the future Bishops of Lincoln and Ely – to be educated.

The eastern part of the bailey was dominated by a large detached kitchen to the south-east of the great hall and was given over to service functions. Apart from the kitchen and its courtyard, little is known about the other buildings and courtyards here, some detached, others against the curtain wall. As the castle would have been self-sufficient, however, a brewhouse, bakery, stabling and servants' accommodation are likely to have been found here. Two gateways provided access: the north-east gate for vehicles, through the outer court, and the north gate, which led to the mere.

❸ WEST RANGE

The two-storey west range abuts the north face of the great tower and faces the south-west gate across the bailey. As first built its exterior was impressive: the internal division of the range into four bays was marked on the exterior walls by pilaster buttresses of honey-coloured stone from Ham Hill (about ten miles away) and its windows were embellished in the same material. The ground floor was originally accessed only from the inner courtyard. An adjacent doorway led to a stair to a first-floor lobby in the tower.

The west range first floor was part of the suite that included the principal apartments on the upper floors of the great tower, to the south, and the bishop's chapel in the north range – the most private part of the castle. Only via the great tower and the north range could the first floor of the west range be accessed, thus creating between these two important buildings a link available only to the more privileged members of the household. At the north end of the west range a two-storey latrine tower projected into the bailey, suggesting domestic apartments occupied this end of the range.

Below right: The south end of the west range abutting the great tower. Adjacent doorways from the inner courtyard opened on to the west range, one giving access to the ground floor, the other to the stair that led to the first-floor lobby of the great tower

A West range

B Great tower

C Great hall west wall

D West walk of inner courtyard

E Entrance to ground floor of the west range

F Entrance to stairway to the first-floor lobby

G Remains of stairway to the first-floor lobby

H Later entrance to the ground floor of the great tower

Below: A 13th-century floor tile from the west range

Left: Roger employed numerous clerks in holy orders at Sherborne. In this detail newly ordained clerks are tonsured by a bishop; French manuscript, c.1390
Below: At Sherborne clerks in holy orders, such as the one depicted here, would have been kept busy with Roger's vast administrative duties; English manuscript, c.1200
Below left: The highly decorated exterior of the window above the altar of the bishop's chapel

A Secular Monastery

Sherborne has been described as a castle throughout its history, but the precise layout of its spacious domestic accommodation suggests otherwise.

It was quite unlike Roger's conventional castle at Devizes, which he entirely rebuilt from about 1113, or the king's castle at Corfe. It was, rather, a fortified palace built on the monastic plan, where the principal buildings – church, refectory, dormitory, chapter house – surround a courtyard, or cloister, which acts as a light well and where roofed walks provide controlled access.

Sherborne replicates this arrangement, even to the extent that the chapels in the north range are aligned east–west and the great tower

parallels the segregated quarters of the abbot. As a bishop, abbot and statesman, Roger led an itinerant life and

none of his properties was his permanent residence: he would visit each regularly, sometimes for only a few days. Sherborne was important because of the valuable Dorset manors that generated so much revenue for the diocese. Clerks in holy orders lived and worked at the castle – some charged with the management and judicial affairs of the estate and others with the upkeep of the palace itself.

Roger's large personal retinue included yet more clergy, whose names appear as witnesses in his charters. In effect, Sherborne was designed for a community of priests dedicated not to prayer and study, but to the administration of the kingdom and the diocese.

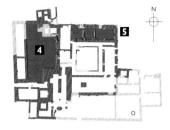

4 WEST COURTYARD

Soon after Bishop Roger's death in 1139 the accommodation at the castle was deemed inadequate; new buildings were added to the south-west of the great tower. These were located in the privileged area of the bailey, without obstructing the fine views over the deer park from the upper floors of the tower, but at the same time were close to the south-west gate.

From the 13th century these new buildings were extended to enclose the area now known as the west courtyard, to the west of the great tower and the west range. A passage from the courtyard to the bailey was created through the buildings on the west side of the courtyard. Opposite this passage a second access to the first floor of the great tower was created by building a stair of two flights on a massive masonry base in the angle between the great and small towers (see page 17). This probably became the principal entrance to the great tower. The lower flight of this stair was widened by Ralegh as part of his modernization from the 1590s.

Probably in the 14th century a doorway was inserted in the outer wall of the west range, allowing access from the courtyard to the ground floor, and on to the inner courtyard.

Some of these west courtyard buildings are completely lost, but the footings of the walls of others remain. The last of them was probably demolished during Ralegh's works.

5 NORTH RANGE

The north range is the most intact of the buildings surrounding the inner courtyard. All the walls survive almost to full height. Externally, the walls retain original window detail and architectural embellishment: the south wall (overlooking the inner courtyard) preserves embellishment similar to the treatment within, while two original windows, with two orders

Below: The buildings at the centre of the bailey seen from the north-west

A North range

B West range

C Area of west courtyard

D Foundations of the west range latrine tower

E Great tower

F Entrance to the west courtyard from the bailey

G Stairway from the west courtyard to the great tower

of chevron moulding supported on columns, remain in the east and north walls. The range was built in four bays. As in the case of the west range, these are defined by pilaster buttresses on the outer wall face.

Internally the walls preserve evidence of their appearance when built. The richness of the architectural detail of the first floor, together with its east–west orientation and direct link via the west range to the upper floors of the great tower, indicate that this space almost certainly formed the bishop's chapel. It is likely that the ground floor formed a lower chapel, serving the less important members of the household.

The ground-floor westernmost bay was barrel-vaulted and probably served as a lobby. It was accessed via doorways from the north walk of the inner courtyard and the north end of the west range and had a circular stair to the first floor. The three bays beyond it, to the east, had groined vaults and formed a single chamber (the ground-floor chapel). There were windows in each bay and at the east end. Local tufa (a type of limestone) was used extensively in the vault construction.

The first-floor plan was similar. The westernmost bay was probably a lobby or ante-chapel reached via the circular stair from below, or through the doorway from the west range (its door jamb remains). The three eastern bays formed a single chamber. Evidence remains of the original impressive architectural treatment, including a dado of blind arcading with intersecting, semicircular arches supported on slender, detached colonnettes.

Above: A reconstruction drawing of the west and north ranges as they may have appeared in about 1130, seen from the north-west. Clerks are at work in the west range, while a service takes place in the lower chapel and, above, Bishop Roger stands at the altar

Below: One of the windows of the bishop's chapel, with the remains of its rich decoration, seen from the inner courtyard

Below: A bishop in procession beneath a canopy borne by clerics. Participants in such formal occasions at the castle would have used the inner courtyard, which was reserved for the most important visitors and residents; English manuscript, c.1400

Bottom: The inner courtyard seen from the south; it forms a square, with each side 50ft (about 15m) long

6 INNER COURTYARD

The striking ruins in the bailey surround an inner courtyard that deliberately resembles a monastic cloister, an innovation in a secular setting that Bishop Roger was one of the first to introduce (see page 9). The courtyard forms a perfect square, with each side 50ft (about 15m) long, located almost exactly at the centre of the bailey, from which it was completely hidden. It was surrounded by four ranges of two-storey buildings and the great tower. Against these buildings, along each side, were arcades. Its central space, or garth, was an open lawn. Only the most important residents and visitors, the members of their households, and the administrators who supported Roger in his role as bishop and statesman had access to this courtyard.

Access to the Courtyard

Originally the only entrance to the inner courtyard from the bailey was via a door at the west end of the south range, or great hall. The great hall itself was entered from the bailey through its south wall at its lower (east) end.

When the west courtyard was built from the 13th century, with its own entrance from the bailey, a second entrance to the inner courtyard was created through the ground floor of the west range (see page 10). Beside this west doorway on to the inner courtyard was the grand stairway, which led from the west walk of the courtyard to a lobby on the first floor of the great tower, and from there to the west and north ranges. Another, smaller stair led from the opposite corner of the courtyard to the upper floor of the east range. A doorway off the north walk led into the lower chapel. It is not known whether there were doors into the ground floor of the east range from the inner courtyard.

Left: Wolvesey Castle, Winchester, the palace built by Henry of Blois, Bishop of Winchester. It was complete by about 1170, with buildings arranged around an inner courtyard, as at Roger's castle at Sherborne
Below: Henry of Blois, Bishop of Winchester and brother of King Stephen; the bishops of England were rich and powerful landowners. Detail of an English manuscript of about 1380

Medieval Bishops' Palaces

William I was zealous in his ecclesiastical reforms and his bishops were rich landholders, ranked as nobility.

With the Norman Conquest, which had the blessing of the Pope, the Church in England grew powerful and influential. William I's bishops were part of an international network headed by the Pope in Rome. Well educated and often well travelled throughout Europe, but with dynastic ambitions theoretically limited by a vow of celibacy, they made invaluable royal administrators.

Within their dioceses, the bishops had important pastoral roles, which took them away from their cathedrals on parish visitations over vast tracts of the country. They had secular business too, since much of their wealth was derived from widely scattered estates, and their presence was needed to ensure effective administration and justice. So palaces were built, like Sherborne, near their estates. It was partly through the building of such palaces, and their cathedrals, that the bishops expressed their power.

Striking examples of their palaces survive and a number remain in use. In the generation after Bishop Roger, Henry of Blois (d.1171), Bishop of Winchester, built a palace at Wolvesey, near his cathedral, and one at (Bishop's) Waltham, about eight miles from

Winchester. Both had a chapel, a strong tower for the principal domestic apartments and a courtyard for controlled circulation. Also built in the 12th century were the three palaces of the Bishops of Lincoln: one at Lyddington, about 45 miles south of Lincoln, which boasted a large hall; another at Buckden, a further 25 miles south, with a great hall and a chapel; and a third built, more conveniently, on the terraces below the cathedral, by Hugh of Avalon (d.1200), Bishop of Lincoln. It had two halls and its own vineyard. Perhaps the grandest remains are those of the vast hall added to the palace at Wells, beside the cathedral, by Richard Burnell (d.1292), Bishop of Bath and Wells.

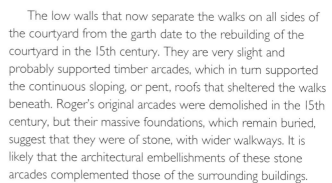

Below: The ground floor of the east range probably provided cellarage for the castle kitchen. In this detail of an Italian manuscript of about 1470 a servant fills a jug with cider

Bottom: The east range seen from the entrance to the stairway to its upper floor

The low walls that now separate the walks on all sides of the courtyard from the garth date to the rebuilding of the courtyard in the 15th century. They are very slight and probably supported timber arcades, which in turn supported the continuous sloping, or pent, roofs that sheltered the walks beneath. Roger's original arcades were demolished in the 15th century, but their massive foundations, which remain buried, suggest that they were of stone, with wider walkways. It is likely that the architectural embellishments of these stone arcades complemented those of the surrounding buildings.

The care and precision with which the castle was planned are clear in the arrangement of this courtyard, in both its symmetry and its role in controlling access and providing light: it allowed the first floors of the surrounding buildings, which had windows in both inner and outer walls, to be flooded with light. These functions, as well as its fine architectural detail, mark out Sherborne as a palace as much as a castle.

▐ EAST RANGE

The east range probably had two socially distinct functions. The barrel-vaulted ground floor had slit windows facing on to the inner courtyard and probably provided cellarage for the kitchen, located immediately to its south-east, beyond the low end of the hall. The upper floor was reached by a stair at the north-east corner of the inner courtyard. A latrine tower originally projected east from the south end of the east wall, suggesting chambers within – probably lodgings for the less important members of the household, who were denied access to accommodation in the great tower.

Castle Supplies

The castle staff was sizeable, and included the steward, clerks, cooks, grooms, masons and soldiers.

The castle community would have varied greatly in size. At its most basic there were scores of people, including the steward or bailiff and clerks responsible for managing the estate, including the deer park and the mere and, during the bishops' ownership, the clerks who administered their estates.

The steward and clerks were supported by domestic staff who cooked the food, grooms who cared for the horses, masons and carpenters who maintained the buildings, soldiers who guarded them, and all their servants. When the king, bishop or important visitors were resident, they and their retinues may at least have doubled the numbers.

The demand for food was unrelenting. Some of this need was met by the mere, where fish and fowl would have been bred, and stored in the north gate once killed. Through the

north-east gate, carts would have delivered grain from local manors held by the bishop or king during their respective periods of ownership. Deer, game and swine would have come from the park and, particularly on great occasions, the manors would have been called upon to provide many score of cattle, delivered on the hoof.

A constant requirement was the maintenance of the buildings. After the initial building, when fine Ham Hill stone, quarried about ten miles away, was used extensively, the stone used to repair and extend the castle was quarried locally, except for the later work by the bishops, which used South Dorset limestone. Timber was always in demand and was sourced either from the bishops' estates or from the royal forests at Gillingham, about 11 miles away .

Top: Three men fishing with nets, as depicted in an English manuscript, c.1310. The mere at Sherborne would have provided fish for the castle kitchen

Middle and above: A man feeds ducks and a waterfowl builds its nest upon the water. Waterfowl would have formed an important part of the diet at Sherborne; details of English manuscripts of c.1200 and c.1310

Above: A reconstruction drawing of the great tower at Sherborne from the south in about 1130, when first built. At this time the only access to the tower was from the west walk of the inner courtyard, via the stairway leading from the ground floor of the west range

8 GREAT TOWER

The massive, three-storey great tower housed the apartments of the principal members of the household. It is rectangular in plan, with walls 10ft (3m) thick. The original entry – the only access – was via a broad curved stairway from the south end of the west walk of the inner courtyard. A door at the base of the stair defended this access; the hole for the drawbar to secure it survives. At the head of the stair a lobby gave access to the first floor of the tower, to the first floor of the west range, and to a circular stair that led up to the second floor of the tower and its parapets.

Originally a spine wall divided the tower, with openings at first-floor level to link the two halves. At second-floor level the spine wall probably supported an arcade. The ground floor could be reached only from the first floor, by a ladder let down through a hole in the floor.

Adjoining the great tower to the west is a smaller square tower, or annexe, which was probably for latrines. In the 13th century a stair was added in the angle between this small tower and the great tower's west face, providing direct access from the west courtyard to the first floor of the great tower.

The original timber upper floors of the great tower were destroyed by a fire, probably in 1450 (see page 32). Between 1485 and 1493 Bishop Langton built stone barrel vaults to carry a new first floor, made extensive additions to the south of the tower, knocked out the spine wall at first- and second-floor levels and added a stair linking the great hall to the tower.

A century later Ralegh demolished most of Langton's work, building a new south wall to the tower with a large compass (semicircular bay) window, which probably reached from the first floor to the roof. He moved a 12th-century column from the second to the ground floor, where it remains today, and widened and added balustrading to the stair on the west side of the tower, making it the principal entrance to his house.

At some point, under Langton or Ralegh, the original stair in the west range was demolished and following this an entrance was created to the ground floor of the great tower in its north wall. Probably only the south wall of the great tower – given the abutting buildings – had windows, though one may have existed in the west wall. Originally they were probably similar to the windows in the south-west gate tower. Despite alterations, the view to the south from the great tower remained unobstructed throughout the history of the castle, presumably because it looked towards the deer park.

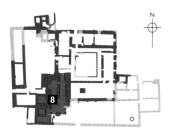

Below: The ground floor of the great tower. The 12th-century column at the centre was moved here from the second floor of the tower by Sir Walter Ralegh in the 1590s

The Coin Hoard

In 1970, during excavation above the vaults of the great tower, 134 coins were found packed together – suggesting they were hidden deliberately by someone intending to recover them. There were 10 gold coins from Spain and Portugal, a silver groat, 2 silver pennies, and 121 silver halfpennies, with a total value equal to that of one of the Spanish gold coins. The hoard was declared treasure trove and acquired by the British Museum in 1971.

The dates and condition of the coins suggest they were concealed in about 1543, shortly after John Leland described the tower in his 1538 *Itinerary*: 'The great lodging is yn the midle of the castle court, very strong and ful of voultes … Bisshop Langeton made of late tyme a new peace of work and lodgings of stone at the west end of the haul.' The date of the hoard confirmed that the vaults had not been disturbed since these works of Langton in the 1480s.

Below: Two of the coins from the hoard of 134 found above the barrel vault of the great tower; left, a gold cruzado of John III of Portugal (r.1521–57) and, right, a silver groat of Edward IV's first reign (1461–70)

9 GREAT HALL

The great hall occupied the south range. It was demolished by Ralegh in the 1590s; its extent is now marked out only by low stone walls. Unusually for the early 12th century the hall was on the ground, rather than the first, floor. It was two storeys high and open to the roof.

The hall was accessed from the bailey through a door in the south wall at the low, or service, end to the east. The west wall, shared with the great tower, preserves the scars of the lateral walls and, between them, the only surviving decorative feature of the interior: a string course carved with a chevron moulding. It is known from excavations that the floor of the great hall was laid with glazed tiles set in a chequer pattern, as were several other of the central buildings, during the 15th century. The dais, or high, end of the hall was at the west end. Here a doorway opened through the north wall on to the south walk of the inner courtyard. Other doorways would have been at the low end, adjoining the kitchen courtyard. The hall was heated throughout its period of use by an open hearth on the central axis, towards the high end. Smoke would have escaped through the windows and a louvre in the roof.

Below: A reconstruction drawing of Sherborne from the south-east in about 1130, showing Bishop Roger arriving with his considerable retinue. Roger is shown, bottom left, drawing up on his horse outside the entrance to the great hall

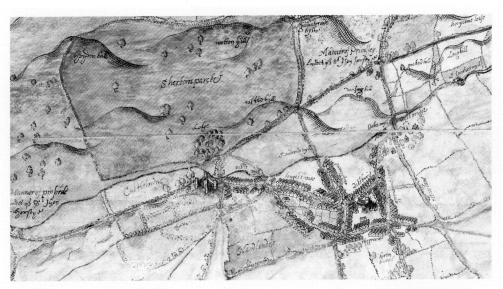

Outer Court

The outer court occupied the area outside the north-east gate and was discovered during excavations in the 1950s.

Nothing of the outer court now survives above ground. It is likely that the buildings there included stables and lodgings for grooms, servants and those not allowed to live within the castle bailey. For this purpose, the outer court is well placed, as the north-east gate was the service entry to the bailey, providing direct access to the rear of the kitchen complex.

There is no evidence of defensive works or enclosure, except that the outer court was within the protective shield of the mere. Excavations revealed three long ranges, aligned east–west, flanking the road to the north-east bridge. From the quality of their construction they appear to date from Bishop Roger's time. One of these buildings probably housed the chapel of St Mary Magdalene, which, at its dedication between 1130

and 1138, was described in a charter issued by Roger as 'visible on the isle where the castle stands'. It would have served the little settlement of tenants and retainers that grew up outside the castle walls.

John Leland's *Itinerary* (1538) mentions this 'chapel in a little close without the castle by este' and an estate map (above) of c.1569–74 shows it in this position. By this date it was standing alone, set apart from the houses of Castleton along the road west of the castle. Ralegh relocated the chapel to its present location in the 1590s. In the 1640s, during the Civil War, the outer court remains were buried beneath an earth bastion built to mount artillery. Later a small summerhouse or hunting box was built on the remains of the bastion for the Earl of Bristol. Today only the bastion mound is visible.

Top: Detail of a map probably commissioned by the Bishop of Salisbury, showing Sherborne estate, c.1569–74. North is at the bottom of the map. Labelled 'St Magdalene's', the chapel in the outer court can be made out just to the left of the castle, and above it the bishop's hunting lodge surrounded by trees

Above and below: *Two extremely rare and important finds from the castle: a gilded copper alloy harness pendant, probably 14th century, with two 'rumbler' bells, which jingled at the movement of the horse; and a matched pair of late 14th- or early 15th-century gilded copper alloy stirrups*

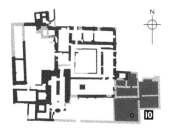

After Bishop Langton's works were complete in about 1493, his enlarged apartments to the south of the great tower were accessed directly from the great hall via a new doorway and connecting stair. The great hall was at the centre of the castle bailey and it would have seen much activity, being used for feasting and formal gatherings as well as for the regular administrative and judicial business of the diocese.

10 KITCHEN AND KITCHEN COURTYARD

Below: A servant with his hands in a tub. Menial activities such as this would have taken place in the castle's kitchen courtyard. Detail of a French manuscript of about 1300

Bottom: The medieval well, with its modern well head, is all that remains of the kitchen and its courtyard; Ralegh demolished the buildings of this service area in the 1590s

The kitchen and its courtyard were demolished by Ralegh in the late 16th century. Only the well, with its modern well head, remains as a visible indication of the southward extent of these buildings. The kitchen, with its hearths and ovens, was a large, rectangular building detached as a precaution against the spread of fire from the east and south ranges. It was originally timber-framed, its roof supported by six square timber posts. It was substantially remodelled, probably more than once, being rebuilt in stone and extended. Under Bishop Langton, between 1485 and 1493, walls were added, linking the kitchen to the great hall and the east range, and a courtyard was built, enclosing the well and connected to Langton's new courtyard south of the great hall.

The kitchen provided food to the south range via the low end of the hall and had access to the storage rooms in the east range. The area between the kitchen and the north-east gate would have been given over to service and storage. It is unlikely that the principal residents of the castle would have been found here. Moreover, the smoke and smells from the kitchen would be blown away from the residential buildings by the prevailing winds from the south-west.

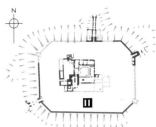

Left: This viewpoint, or 'claire-voie', framed by the east end of the south curtain wall, was created for the Digby family at the end of the 18th century. It overlooks the medieval deer park

⑪ SOUTH CURTAIN WALL

Only fragments remain of the south curtain wall, which was the longest uninterrupted section of the bailey's defence. The dry ditch outside this length of wall is impressively deep. Beyond the ditch is the counterscarp, a bank that originally carried the main Sarum to Sherborne road, and beyond that the ground drops sharply to the mere.

By the end of the 18th century the Sarum–Sherborne road had been moved north of the castle, the prominent crenellated wall had been built along the counterscarp and the landscape between the castle and Ralegh's house within the old deer park had been transformed by Capability Brown (see page 39).

Sherborne Lodge: Ralegh's New Castle

A map of Sherborne, c.1569–74 (see page 19) shows a building labelled 'Lodge' within a grove in the deer park south of the castle. This building formed the core of Ralegh's new house after he abandoned his attempt to modernize the old castle.

John Coker, in his *Survey of Dorset* of 1732, noted that Ralegh 'beganne verie fairlie to builde the castell, but altering his purpose hee built, in a Parke adjoineing to it, out of the Grounde a most fine House, which he beautified with Orchardes, Gardens and Groves of Much Variete and great Deligt'. A later antiquary noted a window pane at Sherborne Lodge bearing Ralegh's armorial shield and the date 1594 – probably the date the Lodge was completed, which suggests Ralegh had given up work on the old castle within two years of acquiring it.

Below: An ink wash drawing of Sherborne Lodge, now known as Sherborne Castle, by Samuel Hieronymus Grimm in 1790. The artist must have been positioned to the north, on the edge of the mere below the old castle

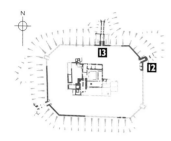

Right: Remains of the north-east gatehouse. The pier in the ditch supported a bridge between the outer court and the bailey

Below: Two caps from gunpowder flasks that would have hung from a bandolier over a soldier's shoulder. They were discarded at the castle during one of the Civil War sieges

Bottom: An 18th-century engraving after an original portrait of Sir Lewis Dyve, the commander of the Royalist garrison during the second siege of Sherborne Old Castle

⑫ NORTH-EAST GATEHOUSE

Only low walls now survive of this gatehouse. It was the main service entrance to the bailey, smaller than the principal entrance through the south-west gatehouse; instead it was similar in size and form to the two curtain wall towers, at the north-west and south-east of the bailey.

The substantial pier and abutments for its bridge, similar to those for the south-west entry, suggest that vehicles could also enter the bailey using this gate. The bridge was probably approached from the east, via a spur off the Sarum–Sherborne

Sherborne in the Civil War

Sherborne was besieged twice during the Civil War. During the final stage of the second siege, on 9 August 1645, John Rushworth, an officer of the Parliamentary forces encamped outside the garrisoned castle, wrote to William Lenthall, Speaker of the House of Commons:
'Wee are very close under their walle, and make good our ground notwithstanding theire many sallyes and throweinge of stones on our heads. The greatest hurte they doe us is by two keepers of parkes they have in the garrison, who in long foulling peeces take aim throughe the loope holes in the wall, for the most part at the commanders … Our peeces can doe noe good on the wall, it being twelve feet thick, but when the great cannon comes it's conceived it will breake down theire towers and doe us great service. It is on the way from Poole … Wee have dismounted all theire old ordnance: beaten them from all four towers, theire great play is throwing down of stoanes I will make no doubt with God's blessige we shall have them every man.'
They did. The Royalist garrison, under the command of Sir Lewis Dyve (left), surrendered six days later.

road that skirted the south side of the castle. On either side of the approach were ranges of buildings forming an outer court. Some of the remains are buried on the far side of the ditch, beneath the prominent mound that once formed an earthwork bastion built to mount artillery to defend the castle during the Civil War.

🖪 NORTH GATE AND BARBICAN

This unusual structure was probably unique in its day. Originally it comprised a large, square, open structure (the barbican) that straddled the dry ditch, and a sloping, vaulted pedestrian passage that ended at the edge of the mere. Although visually impressive, it was originally a weak structure, with very thin walls. Probably later in the 12th century the walls were doubled in thickness, a modification that also provided a wall walk. Later again, under King John (r.1199–1216), round turrets were added to the outer corners to enhance its defences.

The north gate was not a pioneering defensive structure, but a yard with storehouses, probably for game caught on the mere. The mere itself provided the necessary defence on the north flank of the castle. Roger's charter of 1130–38 confirmed the right of Sherborne Abbey's monks to fish in the castle stew ponds, and it seems likely that the mere or part of it served this function. Waterfowl would also have been bred here, so the storehouses within the north gate would have been important for the food supply of the castle. The gate is located slightly to the east of the central axis of the castle and gave direct access to the service sector of the bailey centred on the kitchen.

Gradually the mere silted up. By the time of Bishop Langton in the late 15th century the expanse of water had become boggy ground. With its original purpose gone, the north gate became the postern, or pedestrian entry, which partly remains today. The large, square, 12th-century structure was demolished and replaced by a tower to control access through the curtain wall while the vaulted passage was retained.

Below: Reconstruction drawings of the north gate barbican:

🅰 *c.1130: when the castle was first built*

🅱 *c.1140–1355: the walls have been doubled in thickness and round turrets added to the corners*

🅲 *c.1485–93: the mere has silted up and the barbican has been turned into a postern gate*

Bottom left: The north gate and barbican today from what was once the edge of the mere

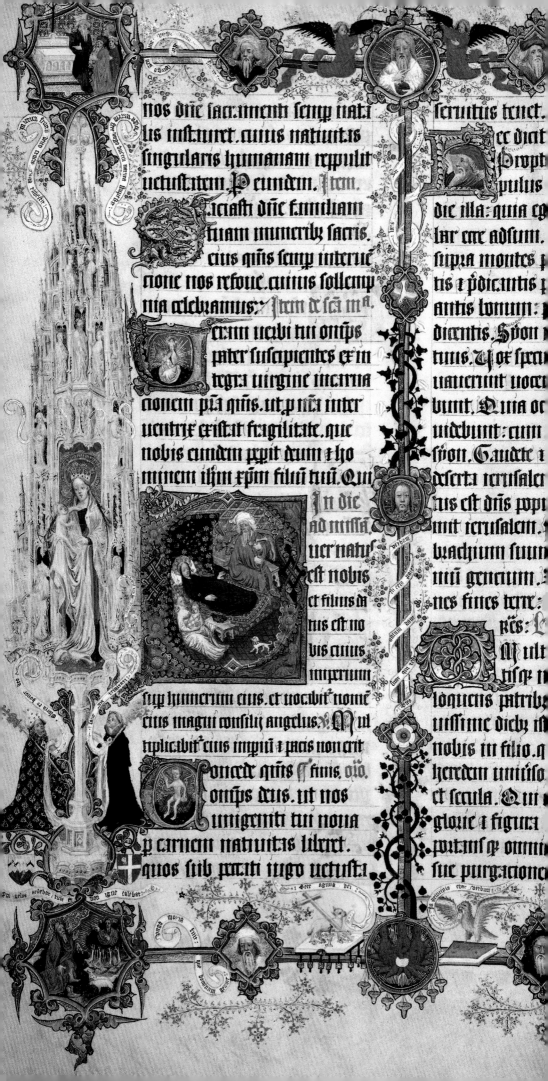

nos dñe sacramenti semp nati
lis instruet. cuius natiuitas
singularis humanam reppulit
uetustatem. P eundem. Item.

...iciasti dñe familiam
tuam muneribz sacris.
eius quos semp interue
cione nos refoue. cuius sollemp
nia celebramus: Item de scã mª.

...erum uerbi tui omps
pater suscipientes ex in
tegra uirgine incarna
cionem pia quis. ut p nrm inter
uentricis exstat fragilitate. que
nobis eundem pepit deum et ho
minem ihm xpm filiu tuu. Qui

In die
ad missã.
uer natus
est nobis
et filius da
tus est no
bis cuius
imperium

sup humerum eius. et uocabit nome
eius magni consilii angelus. ⚜ Mul
tiplicabit eius impiu et pacis non erit
...oncede quis ut finis. oio
omps dñs. ut nos
unigeniti tui noua
p carnem natiuitas liberet.
quos sub peccati iugo uetusta

seruitus tenet.
...ec dicit
...Propt
...pulus
die illa: quia co
...lar ere adsum.
supra montes...
tis et pdicantis...
antis bonum:...
dicentis. Si bon
tinus. Y de spe
uauerint uoce
bunt. Quia oc
uidebunt: cum
...spon. Gaudete et
deserta ierusale
...us est dñs popu
...mit ierusalem.
brachium suum
...niu gencium...
...nes fines terre:
...RCS: L...
...M ult...
...bisq tu...
loquens patrib
...issime diebz is
nobis in filio. q
heredem uniciso
et secula. Q ui
glorie et figura
...portans qp omni
sue purgacione

History of the Castle

BEFORE THE CASTLE

People came to the hilltop site of Sherborne Old Castle about a thousand years before Bishop Roger built here. There is no evidence that they settled here during this period, but Iron-Age and Roman pottery sherds have been found, possibly discarded by travellers on the road that ran through the site.

Anglo-Saxon Burial Ground

During excavation of the castle in 1934, 17 graves were found underlying a rubble foundation beside the great tower. Since then more graves have been found, all either below the level of Roger's castle, or disturbed by those works. Where undisturbed, the graves contained human remains. All had rounded ends and were cut into the rock of the hilltop. The graves were aligned east–west and contained no grave goods, indicating Christian ritual. Analysis of the bones has shown that these are Saxon graves dating to about 640 to 970. Roger's levelling of the site destroyed the evidence that would have given a more precise understanding of the Saxon burial ground but it is probable that a road passed over the hill, linking the important Saxon towns of Shaftesbury and Sherborne, less than a mile away, which was developing over the same period as the burial ground. Burials of a similar period to those at the castle site have been found in the abbey precinct.

Above: A beak-head voussoir (part of an arch or vault) from Roger's castle, reddened by exposure to severe heat. It probably came from the great tower, which was partly destroyed by fire in about 1450
Below: Bishop Aldhelm, first Bishop of Sherborne, founded Sherborne Cathedral in 705. He is depicted here in an English manuscript, c.975–1025
Below left: Sherborne Abbey church, begun in about 1140, as engraved by Daniel King, c.1650

The Diocese of Sherborne

In 705 a diocese was established at Sherborne by Ine, King of Wessex, who appointed Aldhelm (d.c.709) its first bishop, beginning the long association of the medieval Church with Sherborne. Aldhelm founded Sherborne Cathedral, which was served by secular canons. In about 998 the canons were ejected by Bishop Wulfsige, who instead founded a monastery of which he acted as abbot. Aldhelm's original cathedral was expanded in about 1050 and entirely rebuilt from about 1140.

Facing page: A page of the Sherborne Missal, c.1399–1407, from Sherborne Abbey, containing the masses for Christmas Day. On the left are depicted Robert Bruyning, Abbot of Sherborne (in black), and Richard Mitford, Bishop of Sarum (Salisbury)

After the Saxon cemetery fell out of use, in about 970, but before Bishop Roger's time, a ditch was dug to enclose the top of the hill, in the process disturbing some of the graves. Again Roger's later work disturbed any evidence that may have dated this ditch or linked it to other features; only the bottom of the ditch survives in ground later built over. It is likely, however, that the ditch defined the original hilltop, the area later occupied by the west and inner courtyards. When the castle was built the ditch was probably still visible, because massive foundations were built to carry the walls of the great tower across it.

The Norman Conquest

The main impact on Sherborne of the Norman Conquest was the removal in 1075 under Bishop Herman (d.1078) of the bishopric of Sherborne to Sarum. (Sarum, which reached its peak in the 12th century, is now known as Old Sarum and the later town, New Sarum, as Salisbury.) Sherborne did not entirely lose influence as a consequence, however, because Herman's successor, Bishop Osmund (d.1099), and his successor, Bishop Roger, recognized the sizeable contribution to their revenues of the wealthy manors surrounding the town.

Roger was consecrated as Bishop of Sarum in 1107. In 1122 he granted a charter to the monks of Sherborne, separating them from his bishopric and elevating Prior Thurston to the rank of abbot. Probably in the same year he decided to build a defended residence at Sherborne, which was conveniently situated for managing the manors retained by the diocese. The location also had a strategic importance in the western part of the diocese, at the junction of arterial roads in the south-west.

Above: A full-page miniature of St John, c.1150, in the Sherborne Abbey Cartulary, the book in which the monks kept the abbey records
Below: John Leland recorded in 1538: 'The castle of Shireburne is in the east end of the toun, upon a rokky hillet.' This map shows the area at about the time Leland saw it, the 'rokky hillet' of the castle still surrounded by the mere

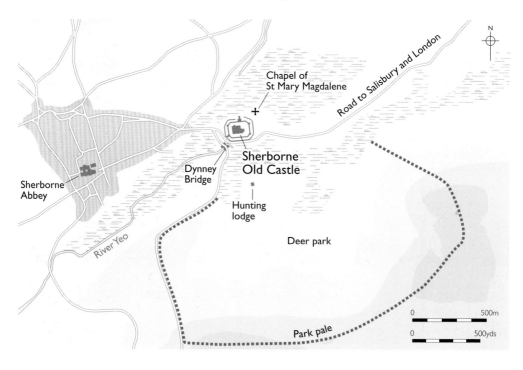

Left: The funeral of William the Conqueror at Caen, Normandy (where Bishop Roger was born). On the right Lanfranc, Archbishop of Canterbury, is shown crowning William Rufus; Netherlandish manuscript illustration, c.1460–68

Sons of the Conqueror

When he died in 1087 William I had three surviving sons: Robert 'Curthose', William 'Rufus' and Henry.

William I spent much of his reign as King of England defending his French dukedom of Normandy. His heir, Robert, chafing for some control of his father's lands, rebelled in 1078. The contemporary chronicler Orderic Vitalis claimed his rebellion was sparked by a joke played on him by his brothers, who emptied a full chamber pot over his head. Their father failed to punish his younger sons and Robert, insulted, laid siege to his father's capital in Normandy. Father and son were sufficiently reconciled, however, for William not to disinherit him. William left Normandy to Robert and England to William Rufus. The youngest, Henry, was left money and bought western Normandy from Robert for £3,000. He was dispossessed

of it, however, in 1091 by his brothers, during one of their rare periods of cooperation.

Immediately after their father's death, a struggle had broken out between Robert and William Rufus. Then in 1095 the Pope issued a call to arms in the Holy Land and Robert set out on the First Crusade. In England the ruthless, unmarried William was not popular, thanks partly to his extension of the royal forests and their punitive laws. His death in the New Forest in 1100 from an arrow shot may not have been accidental. With Robert abroad, Henry at once claimed the throne. Robert returned a month later to find William dead and England under Henry's control.

Unusually for the time, even for the nobility, Henry

had been well educated in Latin and the liberal arts, and his affinity with Roger – highly educated, as typical of his calling – is understandable. Moreover, Roger's position in the king's chapel, the most influential section of the royal household due to the confidential nature of its business, saw his power increase until he was deemed second only to the king.

Conflict between Robert and Henry resumed after Henry's accession and was resolved only at the Battle of Tinchebrai in 1106, when Robert was defeated and taken prisoner. Henry put him in Roger's custody at Devizes Castle (he was moved in 1126 to the custody of Henry's illegitimate son Robert, and died in 1134). But while England now remained relatively quiet, Normandy continued to foment rebellion and Henry spent much of his reign abroad.

Above: A stone carved head of Christ, from Sarum Cathedral, which was entirely rebuilt by Bishop Roger from about 1129. Roger was known by his contemporaries for the 'surpassing beauty' of his buildings
Below: Remains of a small, green-glazed ceramic figurine of a knight from Sherborne Old Castle, dating from the late 13th century. It probably formed part of an aquamanile – a water jug – or possibly a roof finial

THE CASTLE OF BISHOP ROGER

Roger chose a site surrounded by water: a long, low, island-like hill, sloping gently to the west and between the headwaters of the river Yeo. Over the next 15 years his workmen completed his fortified residence to a precise plan, with the walls and windows of the principal buildings embellished with detail carved from Ham Hill stone. The result was a palace of such elegance and obvious expense that it attracted much comment, and not a little envy, from Roger's contemporaries.

Roger's Other Buildings

Roger was known for his building work. Before 1120 he had given his attention to two conventional castles. At Devizes, he rebuilt the castle of his predecessor, Bishop Osmund, which had been destroyed by fire. The contemporary historian Henry of Huntingdon described the outcome, with its formidable defences, as 'the most splendid castle in Europe'.

From about 1129 Roger entirely rebuilt Sarum Cathedral, which was begun by Bishop Herman and finished by Bishop Osmund in 1092. Roger's object was to create a more impressive building; the result was the most magnificent of his projects. At about the same time he remodelled the king's castle at Sarum, of which he was guardian, creating domestic ranges around a courtyard, along similar lines to Sherborne.

William of Malmesbury noted in about 1142: 'At Sarum and Malmesbury … he erected edifices at great cost and with surpassing beauty, the courses of stone being so correctly laid that the joints deceive the eye, and lead it to imagine that the whole wall is composed of a single block.' Of the castle at Malmesbury little is known. In 1216 King John gave permission for its demolition.

THE FALL OF ROGER

Henry I's first wife, Matilda, died in 1118. Two years later his one legitimate son, William Adelin, drowned with the wreck of the *White Ship* off Barfleur, leaving Henry without a male heir. The king immediately took a second wife, Adeliza of Louvain, but the marriage remained childless, so he turned for an heir to his only legitimate daughter, the widowed Empress Matilda (1102–67), and at Christmas 1126 called upon his barons to recognize Matilda as such; it was a bold move to impose a female heir, and one which had opponents from the outset. Roger, however, swore his oath of allegiance to Matilda and the next ten years saw his power and influence flourish. Henry spent as much time in Normandy as in England, and in his absence Roger continued to run affairs in England.

But Henry died suddenly at Lyons-la-Forêt on 1 December 1135, and from then until the accession in 1154 of his grandson Henry II the country would remain in a state of civil war, known as the Anarchy. Despite the king's will that Matilda

Left: A grieving King Henry I depicted above the sinking White Ship, with which his son and heir William Adelin went down in 1120. The disaster led to a state of civil war not resolved until 1154; English manuscript, c.1307–27

Below: A writ of Bishop Roger, dating from between 1136 and 1139, ordering the wife of the Sheriff of Herefordshire to restore her husband's lands to another. At this stage Roger was still very much in power, and managing the affairs of England for King Stephen

inherit, Stephen of Blois (c.1097–1154), son of Henry's sister Adela, claimed the throne. To Stephen, Roger's support was crucial – it would bring with it the whole of the financial and administrative management of England – and he persuaded Roger to back him. By 22 December Roger was one of three prelates assisting in Stephen's coronation at Westminster, despite his earlier oath of allegiance to Matilda.

For the next three years, including some months when Stephen was in Normandy, Roger managed the king's affairs, as he had those of Henry. But Stephen grew to mistrust Roger, encouraged by the many who envied his position, and in June 1139 events moved quickly. Fearing Roger meant to transfer his allegiance to Matilda, Stephen summoned him to his court in Oxford. Roger went, with his son (with his mistress Matilda of

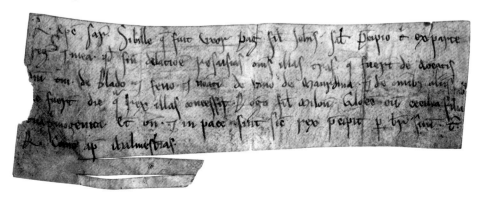

Above: A marble tomb slab thought to be that of Bishop Roger. It was one of three bishops' tombs moved from the cathedral at Old Sarum in 1226 to the new cathedral at Salisbury, where it remains

Right: A reconstruction drawing of the great tower from the south, c.1190. The buildings to the left of the tower were added earlier in the century, after the castle was taken into possession of the Crown, probably to make the bishop's lodgings more appropriate for secular use

Ramsbury) Roger, who was the king's chancellor, and two of his nephews: Nigel, Bishop of Ely, and Alexander, Bishop of Lincoln. Roger and his son were arrested. Nigel escaped to Devizes Castle, where Matilda of Ramsbury resided. The king, with Roger and his son in his custody, besieged Devizes Castle and, having shut Roger up in a cowshed, threatened to hang his son, at which Nigel and Matilda surrendered. In July Stephen seized Roger's castles of Sherborne, Malmesbury and Sarum. In August Roger's trial opened at Winchester and in December, a broken man, he died at Sarum, aged about 74 years.

A ROYAL CASTLE

Sherborne remained with the Crown for two centuries after its seizure by Stephen in 1139, and thanks to excellent records of expenditure – the Pipe Rolls – following Roger's reforms of the Treasury, a good deal is known about what happened here.

In 1143 Stephen surrendered the castle to Robert, 1st Earl of Gloucester, an illegitimate son of Henry I. In 1183, after the death of William, 2nd Earl of Gloucester, Henry II (r.1154–89) resumed ownership of the castle. As Sherborne was planned for use by a bishop and his household, it is unlikely to have provided suitable accommodation for a secular family. Soon buildings were added between the south-west gatehouse and the great tower, located so as not to obscure the view from the tower over the deer park. They are known only from excavation, and were demolished and replaced by the west courtyard ranges in the late 13th century.

The earliest expenditure in the Pipe Rolls is for 100 shillings for repairs to the great tower, when the castle was held by Richard I (r.1189–99). King John (r.1199–1216) visited the castle three times and his first wife, Isabella of Gloucester, stayed

here in 1207–8; in 1208 John had the 'lodgings' repaired. In 1215, doubtless prompted by the baronial uprisings, he upgraded the defences, paying particular attention to the north gate.

As early as the 1160s the 'king's houses' at Sherborne are referred to in the royal Itinerary, and in the 1250s separate lodgings and chapels for the king and the queen are mentioned when Henry III (r.1216–72) ordered repairs: 'We command you to make a fireplace in the Queen's chamber in the castle of Sherborne, and a certain penthouse from the door of that chamber to the door of the same Queen's chapel.' The king went on to direct repairs to the roof, north wall, tower, various doors and windows, and to 'the glass windows in our chapel so that they may be shut and opened'. These repairs were not done immediately. A survey of 1261 describes the castle as 'in a ruinous state' and notes the rusting armour stored there.

The west courtyard and the stair from it to the great tower were probably built before Henry III's second son, Edmund, Earl of Lancaster, was appointed governor of the castle in 1267. Edmund's brother, Edward I (r.1272–1307), stayed at Sherborne on at least three occasions. Part of the outer court was at this time in use as a prison: ten Welsh hostages, probably taken during Edward I's campaign in Wales in 1295, were held there in that year at a daily cost to the Treasury of 4 pence.

DISPUTES OF OWNERSHIP

In 1330 Edward III (r.1327–77) granted Sherborne to its constable, William Montagu, whom he created Earl of Salisbury in 1337. This shift of ownership out of royal hands offered a possibility to the diocese, now relocated at New Sarum, or Salisbury, to reclaim the castle: for a bishop could sue a fellow nobleman, but not the king. In 1337 Bishop Robert Wyvil (d.1375) unsuccessfully applied for a licence to crenellate the castle. In 1355 he became more forceful, applying for a writ against the 2nd Earl of Salisbury on the grounds that the Crown had relinquished its immediate interest in the castle, which remained integral to the bishops' Sherborne estate.

The earl chose to settle the matter in a trial by combat. As a clergyman, Wyvil was prohibited from fighting, so he appointed a champion. Nor did the earl want to fight in person, and did likewise. In the event, the earl's champion failed to turn up and the bishop's champion was declared the victor. Behind the scenes, however, the bishop had agreed to pay 2,500 marks to the earl and 500 marks to the king for the return of the castle.

Wyvil's success gave him considerable personal satisfaction. In 1357 he entertained Edward III's eldest son, the Black Prince, at Sherborne. Wyvil's memorial brass in Salisbury Cathedral depicts a bishop in his vestments standing with uplifted hands within the walls of an elaborate castle, while below him his armed champion bars the way through the castle gate.

Above: William Montagu, 2nd Earl of Salisbury, as depicted in the Bruges Garter Book, c.1430. The earl lost Sherborne to Bishop Wyvil in 1355 after a trial by combat

Below: A drawing of the memorial brass, c.1375, to Bishop Robert Wyvil in Salisbury Cathedral, celebrating his successful reclamation of Sherborne. Wyvil stands triumphant, with his champion below

Above: An iron spur with the remains of a six-pointed rowel, or goad, found at Sherborne. It is typical of spurs of the mid 14th century, and would originally have been covered in tin and polished to a shine

THE BISHOPS' WORKS

In 1377 Bishop Ralph Ergham renewed attempts to get a licence to crenellate, but little else is known of the early years of the castle after its return to the bishops. Its main use in the diocese, however, reverted to that intended by Roger: an administrative centre for the local estates and a residence during visitations. Given the extensive enlargements during royal ownership, the diocesan clerks must have been accommodated lavishly. Except for the enclosure of the south courtyard, the bishops did no building work for over a century after regaining the castle.

In about 1450 the castle was plundered by disaffected local inhabitants (see below). Severe scorch marks in the great tower indicate a fire, probably caused at this time, which destroyed the timber upper floors. But as the tower was probably not needed for diocesan business, it was neglected. Then, in the 1480s, Bishop Thomas Langton took up residence. The trend at the time was towards smaller, more private domestic apartments and Langton began a radical modernization, while retaining the castle's medieval form. He demolished Roger's inner courtyard arcades, rebuilding them in a lighter, more fashionable style, and relaid the floor of the great hall with glazed tiles set in a chequered pattern. In the great tower he removed the dividing spine wall on the first floor and arcade on

Murder of the Bishop

In 1450 disaffection over the unpopular Henry VI (r.1422–61; 1470–71) turned into an uprising. In June rebels marched on London led by one Jack Cade, whose manifestos declared corrupt, among others, William Aiscough, Bishop of Salisbury – a member of Henry VI's inner circle and his personal confessor.

Aiscough fled London for the safety of Sherborne Castle, but his baggage train was plundered and on 29 June, some 30 miles short of Sherborne, he

Right: On his way to Sherborne in 1450 the Bishop of Salisbury was stabbed to death during a popular uprising. In a similar uprising 70 years earlier the Archbishop of Canterbury was murdered (depicted here in a Netherlandish manuscript, c.1475)

was dragged from a church where he was celebrating Mass and was stabbed to death. In the days following, Sherborne and several other of the bishop's manors were ransacked, his

diocesan records destroyed and 10,000 marks-worth of property was said to have been stolen. Jack Cade's Rebellion was defeated in a battle on London Bridge on 6 July 1450.

Left: A reconstruction drawing of the great tower from the south, c.1480. By this time the west courtyard had been enclosed, the lodgings added to the great tower in the 12th century being demolished in the process, and the courtyard south of the great hall had been created

Below left: A reconstruction drawing of the great tower a few years later, in about 1493, after the completion of Bishop Thomas Langton's considerable modernization

Below: The west bay of the ground floor of the great tower. The stone barrel vaulting was added by Bishop Langton during his tenure, between 1485 and 1493

the second, creating large open rooms at both levels. Over the two ground-floor bays he built barrel vaults to carry a new stone floor at a higher level than the destroyed wooden one. To the south front of the tower he added a chamber block lit by an oriel (projecting bay) window, probably having driven large openings through the original wall. To link this new block to the great hall he built a stair, also lit by an oriel window, in the angle of the tower and the great hall. Finally, he altered the kitchen area and, probably because the mere was already 'chokid up with flagges and wedes', as John Leland noted in his 1538 *Itinerary*, he demolished the courtyard of the north gate and replaced it with the tower that survives as a ruin today.

Above: Portrait of Sir Walter Ralegh by William Segar, dated 1598, when Ralegh was living at Sherborne. The following year Ralegh persuaded Elizabeth I to allow him to buy the freehold of the castle outright

WALTER RALEGH AT SHERBORNE

In 1542 Dorset, which had formed part of the Diocese of Salisbury, was transferred to the newly created Diocese of Bristol. The bishops of Salisbury retained Sherborne Castle, but with the reduction in the area of the diocese it was no longer required for ecclesiastical purposes. For most of the next 50 years they leased the castle and its estates to the Crown.

Sir Walter Ralegh (1554–1618) had been impressed by the decaying buildings and their surroundings while travelling from Plymouth to the court at Westminster and in 1592 he convinced Elizabeth I (r.1558–1603) to transfer the lease to him and his heirs in perpetuity. In 1599 he purchased the freehold.

Ralegh initially attempted to modernize the large, neglected, medieval palace, unchanged since Langton's work a century earlier. The archaeological evidence suggests that Ralegh demolished more than he built. The great hall in the south range, Langton's chamber block to the south of the great tower and the kitchen were all swept away. The outer court, which had developed into a village known as Castleton by at least 1536, was demolished and rebuilt to the west of the castle.

Ralegh then focussed his attention on the great tower. Here he set out to build, but may not have completed, a new south wall with a compass window reaching from the first floor to the height of the roof, and a grand, balustraded entrance stairway to the first floor from the west courtyard. In the bailey only works to the south-west gatehouse were completed. Court papers show that Ralegh's former steward John Meere, who sued Ralegh in 1601, lived there, although Ralegh described the

Above: The Dianthus caryophyllus, *or Clove pink, growing on the castle walls. These sweet-scented flowers are known locally as 'Lady Betty's Pinks', after Bess Throckmorton, Ralegh's wife, who it is said introduced the flowers to Sherborne*

Sir Walter and his Wife

Ralegh was an adventurer, poet, courtier and scholar. He came from an established family in east Devon and, after a successful career as a soldier in Ireland, found his way to Elizabeth I's court, where he attracted her attention, became a favourite, and was knighted and made captain of her guard in 1591.

Privateering Ralegh family connections in the West Country helped Ralegh in his desire to explore the New World; he was continually involved in expeditions, but his ambition of finding riches – particularly gold – remained unfulfilled.

In 1592, shortly after gaining the lease of Sherborne, Ralegh's secret marriage to Elizabeth (Bess) Throckmorton, one of the queen's maids of honour, became known to Elizabeth I. The couple were banished from court. He regained favour with Elizabeth I, but his arrogance, extravagance and rumoured atheism brought him enemies, and after the queen's death in 1603 he was unjustly arrested for treason and kept in the Tower of London until 1616. Then, in 1618, after another failed expedition to South America, he was rearrested and beheaded on the orders of James I.

castle at this time as 'altogether uninhabitable'. For whatever reason – possibly financial – Ralegh early on abandoned work at the castle and shifted his attention to its early 16th-century hunting lodge in the deer park south of the lake. He rebuilt the lodge as a country house, which was largely complete by about 1594. A survey of 1600–1609 shows it as Ralegh left it: a rectangular building with octagonal corner turrets.

In 1603, after the death of Elizabeth I, Ralegh was arrested for treason. His wife, Bess Throckmorton, was permitted to keep Sherborne until 1608, when James I (r.1603–25) bought the estate from her and gave it, firstly, to the Earl of Somerset, and then to his son Henry, Prince of Wales.

Above left: The ruins of Sherborne Old Castle seen across the lake from the grounds of Ralegh's lodge, now the new castle

Above: Reverse and obverse of a silver threepenny coin of Elizabeth I found at Sherborne and dated 1572

Below left: A reconstruction drawing of the castle as modernized by Ralegh in the 1590s: he demolished much of the medieval palace and began, though may not have finished, the transformation of the great tower

Below: A copper alloy belt buckle found at Sherborne, dating from 1550 to 1650. It may have been worn by one of Ralegh's household, or perhaps a soldier during one of the sieges of the Civil War

Above: John Digby, Baron Digby of
Sherborne and 1st Earl of Bristol, in
1628, by Cornelius Johnson. Digby
bought the Sherborne estate from
the king in 1617
Below: Portrait of William Seymour,
Marquess of Hertford, attributed to
Gilbert Jackson. Hertford commanded
the Royalist garrison at the first siege
of Sherborne Old Castle in 1642

SHERBORNE IN THE 17TH CENTURY

In 1617 James I sold the Sherborne estate to Sir John Digby
(1580–1653), his ambassador to Spain, for £10,000. Digby was
created Baron Digby of Sherborne in 1618 and Earl of Bristol in
1622, after which he retired to Sherborne. There he enlarged
Ralegh's house, then known as Sherborne Lodge, by adding a
wing at each corner.

The Civil War: the First Siege of Sherborne

During the Civil War the castle was twice besieged. Lord
Bristol allowed the old castle to be garrisoned for the king and
in August 1642 a Royalist force, under the command of William
Seymour, Marquess of Hertford, made repairs to the castle
defences in anticipation of attack. Parliamentary forces, under
William Russell, Earl of Bedford, approached and encamped on
the high ground to the north. On 4 September they attacked,
only to be seen off by a battery of field-gun fire from the
castle. The siege dragged on, however, until 20 September,
when Hertford surrendered and was allowed to withdraw.
Parliamentary commissioners occupied the castle until they
were evicted four months later by a small Royalist force.

The Civil War: the Second Siege of Sherborne

Charles I (r.1625–49) and his nephew Prince Rupert reviewed
their troops at the castle on 2 October 1644 and ate a picnic
lunch in the deer park. In August 1645 Sherborne – 'a malicious
mischievous Castle, like the owner', according to Oliver
Cromwell – was again besieged. Sir Lewis Dyve, the Earl of
Bristol's stepson and the local Royalist commander, held the
castle against Parliamentary forces led by Cromwell and
Sir Thomas Fairfax. Dyve, with 150 soldiers and some cavalry,
held out for 11 days despite artillery bombardment, mining and
being forced to retreat into the great tower.

Parliamentary officers were killed and wounded by sniper
fire from the estate gamekeepers and found it 'a difficult peece
of worke', as recorded by one (see page 22). But on 15 August
1645 Dyve surrendered, and he and his wife, 3 MPs, 3 colonels,
23 officers, 55 gentlemen, and 344 soldiers gave up the castle
and were all sent by ship to London as prisoners. The castle
goods were sold off at the local market and Parliament
ordered the castle to be slighted to prevent it being used again
as a Royalist stronghold. Much of what had survived the siege
was demolished that October. Bristol, who had been in Exeter
since the previous year, went to France. In 1648 he and his son
George were formally banished.

Following the restoration of Charles II (r.1660–85), George
Digby (1612–77), 2nd Earl of Bristol, returned from France and
reclaimed the estate. His son John, the 3rd Earl, died without
an heir in 1698 and the title became extinct. Sherborne passed
to a cousin, William (1661–1752), 5th Baron Digby.

Excavations and Finds at Sherborne Old Castle

Despite early antiquarian interest in the castle, excavations only began in the 20th century.

The first attempt to produce a plan of Sherborne was by the castle scholar GT Clark in 1874. It was not until 60 years later that excavation began, under the local amateur archaeologist and surveyor for Sherborne Urban District Council, Charles Bean (1892–1983), supported by the estate owner, Colonel Frederick Wingfield Digby (1885–1952). Bean's explorations lasted until 1954. He examined most of the bailey and part of the outer court, and brokered the transfer of the castle's care to the Ministry of Works in 1956.

By this time the ruins were in a state of near collapse, and further excavation was not possible until they were repaired. From 1967 until the 1990s the Ancient Monuments Inspectorate undertook further excavations to set out the site for public display.

There have been some outstanding finds, including a large collection of carved 12th-century stonework that once embellished Bishop Roger's original castle; a coin hoard of the 1540s (see page 17), which enabled the dating of alterations to the great tower; and much pottery, metalwork and bones, both human and animal, which have provided information about the site and the life in the castle. Some of these objects are on display at Sherborne (new) Castle.

Top: Sherborne Old Castle under excavation on 11 March 1958

Above right: *A copper alloy and gilt heart-shaped clasp, set with amethysts, found at the castle. It is probably Victorian and appears to be a love token*

Above: *This copper alloy thimble, probably of the 18th century, was found at the castle – possibly dropped by someone visiting the ruins*

Above: William, 5th Baron Digby, in 1715, by Godfrey Kneller. William inherited Sherborne in 1698 and his son Robert improved the gardens

Below: The picturesque ruins of the old castle from the east in 1785, by Robert Sherburne. From the 1730s views of the castle show it as ivy-clad ruins, among which cattle graze

A ROMANTIC RUIN

In 1724 the poet and essayist Alexander Pope visited Robert (c.1692–1726), the 5th Baron's second son, who had created a formal layout of canals and lawns, depicted on an estate map of 1732, to the north of Sherborne Lodge. Pope wrote to a friend of the beauty of the park and continued: 'What should induce my Lord Digby [the 5th Baron] the rather to cultivate these ruins and to do honour to them is that they do no small honour to his family … the adorning and beautifying of them in the manner I have been imagining would not be unlike the Egyptian finery of bestowing ornaments and curiosity on dead bodies.'

In 1752 Edward (1730–57), William's grandson, became the 6th Baron Digby and the following year consulted Lancelot 'Capability' Brown. Following Brown's advice a lake was created in the deer park with a cascade below the old castle. The view was also opened up to the north of the Lodge, with the castle as a romantic eye-catcher, enhanced by the addition in 1755 of a crenellated wall along the old south defences and, in 1756, of a new 'ruined' round tower higher up the castle hill to the east. In 1789–90 Henry (1731–93), 7th Baron Digby, had a tunnel and driveway built for carriages to pass from the park into the castle bailey. From account books we know that works were carried out to maintain the fabric of the old castle until the 1790s.

THE CASTLE TODAY

Sherborne Old Castle remains much as it was when left ruined on Parliament's orders in 1645. An engraving of 1733 by the Buck brothers depicts more of the curtain wall standing, but little else has changed; Bishop Roger's buildings proved enduring, both physically and functionally – unlike the castle's environment. Beyond the counterscarp bank few features

Landscapes of Lancelot 'Capability' Brown

Sherborne was among Brown's early commissions, and remains one of the most intact.

In March 1753, Edward, 6th Baron Digby of Sherborne, sought a landscape gardener to redesign the park. It was to Lancelot 'Capability' Brown (1716–83) that he turned.

In 1741 Brown had been appointed by Viscount Cobham to work at Stowe, his estate in Buckinghamshire, under William Kent. He went on to develop a large practice, creating more than 170 gardens, landscapes and buildings. His reliance on highly skilled foremen enabled him to undertake several commissions at the same time.

By the 1730s formal gardens, dominated by lawns, canals and geometric shapes, had fallen out of fashion. There was a new enthusiasm for enhancing the natural features of the landscape. By the end of the 18th century this fashion gave way to a taste for the untamed Picturesque landscape.

Brown's clients used their estates for various activities, such as forestry, agriculture and sport, and he skilfully disguised these functions by the use of sunken fences, or ha-has, and water diverted and dammed to form streams and lakes to create working, but apparently natural, landscapes. On his advice the formal gardens at Sherborne were removed and the lake and vista taking in the castle ruins created north of the Lodge. In 1776 he built a ha-ha along the east lawn, hiding the carriage drive, and created the lakeside gardens, which, according to the contract, he planted with 'trees, shrubs and flowers'.

Above: The grounds of Sherborne Castle in 1785, by Robert Sherburne, after 'Capability' Brown had completed his transformation of the landscape. The bridge, which remains today, was built in 1767–9 to designs by Robert Digby (1732–1815), a brother of the 6th Baron Digby

Below: A portrait of Lancelot 'Capability' Brown by Richard Cosway, c.1770–75

remain from before the Civil War. Among them are Dynney
Bridge, within the grounds of Sherborne Castle, built by Roger
to command the junction of the main highways from the castle,
the Civil War bastions, and the deer park to the south. The
surrounding mere and the outer court of Roger's castle now
form, to the east, fields and to the west, a cluster of houses and
the church of Castleton village, removed there by Ralegh. To
the south, although the deer park remains intact, the episcopal
hunting lodge of the early 16th century is now Sherborne
Castle, surrounded by the 'Capability' Brown landscape.

The aspect to the north has seen the greatest change. The
mere on the headwater of the river Yeo now forms pasture
fields bisected by the railway. Originally, to those approaching
the castle from the north across the mere, the north gate,
with the mass of the great tower behind it, would have risen
up from an expanse of water: striking, near-impregnable and
a vivid display of Bishop Roger's power.